TRUE HEART, SOLID BOUNDARIES

Spiritual Self-Care for Healing Your Inner Child
and Empowering Your Authentic Self

CATHERINE GERDES

BALBOA.PRESS
A DIVISION OF HAY HOUSE

Balboa Press books may be ordered through booksellers or by contacting:

Balboa Press
A Division of Hay House
1663 Liberty Drive
Bloomington, IN 47403
www.balboapress.com
844-682-1282

Because of the dynamic nature of the Internet, any web addresses or links contained in this book may have changed since publication and may no longer be valid. The views expressed in this work are solely those of the author and do not necessarily reflect the views of the publisher, and the publisher hereby disclaims any responsibility for them.

The author of this book does not dispense medical advice or prescribe the use of any technique as a form of treatment for physical, emotional, or medical problems without the advice of a physician, either directly or indirectly. The intent of the author is only to offer information of a general nature to help you in your quest for emotional and spiritual well-being. In the event you use any of the information in this book for yourself, which is your constitutional right, the author and the publisher assume no responsibility for your actions.

Any people depicted in stock imagery provided by Getty Images are models, and such images are being used for illustrative purposes only. Certain stock imagery © Getty Images.

Print information available on the last page.

ISBN: 978-1-9822-5719-4 (sc)
ISBN: 978-1-9822-5721-7 (hc)
ISBN: 978-1-9822-5720-0 (e)

Library of Congress Control Number: 2020921120

Balboa Press rev. date: 11/04/2020

This if for the buriers.

For the people pleasers.

For the (over)doers and (over)givers.

I see you.

Contents

Introduction:
When the Blinders Came Off

To be nobody but yourself in a world which is doing
its best, day and night, to make you like everybody else
means to fight the hardest battle which any human being
can fight ... It takes courage to grow up and become who
you really are.
—e. e. cummings

When I was seventeen, my dad suddenly passed away from a heart attack. My grieving from his spirit leaving his body felt compounded by regret over the relationship as it had never been. At times throughout those seventeen years, I had trouble feeling emotionally close with him and the painful memories often overshadowed the loving ones. I felt regret and shame around not having the opportunity to mend these old wounds and resolve the hurts left unspoken. In a larger sense, I felt like the opportunity for mending and for his love had been abruptly taken away. Eventually, I believed a silent and sabotaging lie—this loss was somehow a reflection of what I deserved.

Being raised a girl in the South, there was a rampant subtly ingrained cultural message: I couldn't take up too much space, and it was my inherent responsibility to care for others. This showed up in the forms of people-pleasing or over-giving, which was the breaking of some of my self-honoring boundaries. At times, I believed that love looked like incessant giving in my relationships with uneven expectations for reciprocity.

I carried my worthiness wounds or made-up mantle of caretaker around in future negotiations, relationships, and friendships, where I often opened emotional space for others at the cost of suppressing my own feelings.

As an adult, I unconsciously used the vibrant impenetrable noise and activity of New York City to quiet a more substantial cry for more—more heart-healing and authentic love. There was an outward fearlessness covering up a quiet fearfulness, which felt easy to internally bypass in a loud city. This quiet ticking, signaling a desire for cultivating greater compassion for myself, had been chiming away. At different points—and sometimes to the advantage of others—I believed that lie that I couldn't take up much space. A long, uncomfortable, and unsustainable habit became suppression.

In my thirties, I finally came to see this worthiness wound for what it was. I know now this was an imposter hiding my truth and authenticity.

In my thirties, just after the start of this awakening, my mom was diagnosed with dementia. After seventeen years, I returned to live in my hometown of Wilmington, North Carolina, from New York City. I soon learned that my childhood wounds were fresher than I realized, and my inner cry for more grew louder. I grew more aware of these unprocessed feelings and the heartbreak of my dad's passing. When I allowed myself to truly feel it again, I started a longer-than-anticipated journey of actively feeling, releasing, and healing. I grew more honest with myself about these repressed feelings. I forgave myself for glossing over and bypassing my own feelings and not accepting my own worthiness. I forgave my family for what was left unresolved too.

Returning offered me the opportunity to heal old wounds that I thought had healed. In facing my childhood again, processing through that old pain *and* old love, I now had the chance to retell myself the story that integrates both and is truer. I came home to my own wholeness through my breaking, and what felt like a collapsing of the pieces was a falling back into place and arrival back home to my authentic self. I was healing my inner child.

If you experienced some form of trauma in your childhood and live in America, you are in the majority. For those of us who have endured any form of childhood trauma, or for those grieving a loss, sometimes the pressures from messages like "vibe higher" or an external expectation to abruptly move forward can feel insensitive and unrealistic. These messages do not always apply the same way for us.

For those who have experienced any form of trauma, putting in the work to heal and move forward by looking back calls for celebration. The work is messy, tiring, and cannot be done on someone else's timetable. It impacts not just our minds and hearts, but can also be stored away and locked inside our bodies.

Once I allowed myself to feel shame and actively work through my blockages, I experienced the opportunity to feel, process, and release through forgiveness as the pathway to freedom. Covering almost two years, it took longer than I would have expected. And, I had to continually forgive myself and others. But freeing myself could be and was my choice, as long as I allowed for it and surrendered to the process.

I found truth for myself in both sides of some contradictions. The messages to not reside in victimhood, but to also not suppress, resonated for me. The concept of moving forward *and* also looking back was healing. When in doubt, listen to your body and ask it for guidance. No one can project onto you how long your healing process should take, or what you feel unless you allow for it.

Listen to your body. Feeling chronic tightness or exhaustion can allude to emotional grasping onto old wounds that have manifested into symptomatic form. An inability to stay present in the moment may indicate a need to resolve—even, internally—an unresolved issue that has proven mentally draining. The sweeping under the rug of emotional residue is not sustainable. This residue can come up later in the form of triggers.

Inner-Child Healing Affirmations
for Healing Codependency

- I am waking up to my own worthiness.
- I am accepting that another person's behavior does not reflect my inherent value.
- I am allowing myself to give back to myself.
- I am accepting that prioritizing my needs is not selfish.
- I am no longer apologizing for or belittling my truth.
- I am using my voice, even when it disturbs another's peace.
- I am accepting that in order to be effective, I must prioritize myself.
- I am allowing for unconditional love to enter.
- I am giving love to myself.

When my inner wounds were in the process of coming into high relief, I more readily recognized the wounding around me. In some cases, others mirrored back to me my own residual wounding. I began noticing repetition compulsion, or cyclical patterns, in some of my past relationships. I began spotting other codependent adults with hurting inner children holding onto the hope of finding healing in another wounded partner. Now, I could hear attachment mistaken for love. I heard this attachment called *love* coursing through song lyrics that used to resonate with me.

While my former home of Wilmington had changed some, I had transformed more than I recognized. Returning home provided an unconsciously sought out litmus test of how much I had changed—my former self was apologetic in her energy and her stance. Meanwhile, my more authentic and bold self had transitioned from bud to blossom. My view of the world, my view of myself, and my view of women and the unequal responsibilities placed upon them had all changed.

Along this old southern path, I embraced my own evolution and had encounters with women reflecting a younger people-pleasing version of myself. While not limited to the south, this cultural expectation of fawning, or excessive emotional giving, is loud here. Just as I was subtly culturally taught to put others first and suppress my needs or desires, I witnessed another generation being subtly socially groomed too. Two decades later, this learned behavior was reflected back to me through a new group of southern women.

And now, the blinders were gone. I witnessed how a woman's behavior makes others feel is considered more important than how she actually feels. I identified the prioritization of superficial bubbliness over genuine authenticity. It seemed like a woman's worth was being measured by her ability to be in a constant state of happy rather than a free state of authenticity. I learned that suppression was the norm. It is heartbreaking to watch young women suppress and conform, even in their energy and posture. Witnessing ingenuine responses to unwanted advances or a frequent directive to "just smile" are easy to find. No matter the geography, the genuine expression of a woman's truth interpreted as either too emotional or *too much* is rampant. In these ways, coming home felt like returning to the '50s.

This cultural ingraining and early message to play small in my own life was showing up in high relief. An illusion of safety created by not rocking the people-pleasing boat had, at different times, kept me stagnant. Now, this belief was screaming to be acknowledged and shed more. Unknowingly, my hidden wounds around a perceived unworthiness had been pulling the strings throughout my youth and young adulthood.

In different ways, I had been compartmentalizing myself within my own story. Over a nearly two-year course of doing the work to heal, I surrendered to the truth of these patterns. I followed the inner nudge guiding me to heal. I acknowledged that, at times in my past, I had been hooking my hope onto a star that someone else got to set. A wounded part of me had set the bar for lower expectations and silenced myself in the part of the conversation where I could have taken more space. As codependents tend to do, I carried the emotional responsibilities of others. Sometimes, this provided distraction from my own healing and felt like a default from my conditioning.

In this town that I had associated with abandonment, I am grateful I was shown my wounds more vividly in order to heal them. Where I didn't know I needed to return wound up being a messy haven for my cocooning. It became a retreat of rediscovering myself. Along this journey, I changed the way I valued my body and my mind. My habits and my diet shifted. I invested my time differently and became more conscious of the information I consumed. I turned toward cultivating a deeper spiritual practice that included treating my body as a temple and actively healing through some of the steps I've outlined in this book. I surrendered to the healing practice of meditation for letting go and allowing in.

Self-soothing and transformational healing happens across all parts of ourselves – mind, body and soul. The metamorphosis from playing small and expanding more fully includes healing beliefs, healing our relationship with ourselves, and opening up the possibility for transformation in our relationships.

Once we actively heal, we can shed lies that we have given the title of truths, integrate the layers of our past, and rewrite our authentic story. Facing the reality of who we are and shedding falsely held beliefs, we can finally see ourselves. On the other side of this healing journey *through* our feelings lies self-acceptance.

If you are going through your own dark-night-of-the-soul journey, you are not alone. If you are starting to recognize that you have unhealthy patterns or just beginning to see a cycle that you are ready to break for yourself, welcome.

In the pages that follow, the focus is on all interconnected parts of you along with steps you can take to reconnect with your inner strength, release stored-away emotions, and arrive home within yourself. Through steps you actively take to heal, you are not alone on your journey. You are actively cocreating and healing with the Divine.

This path is intended to purge an old version of yourself that doesn't line up with who you genuinely are designed to be—one that served others but no longer sustainably and lovingly serves yourself. Dedication to the route of healing is producing who you are meant to be: an authentic you.

The Path Forward

Be kind and gentle with yourself.

Truths for People-Pleasers to Embrace

- It is not selfish to take care of your needs.
- You can set healthy boundaries *and* have loving relationships.
- Pay attention when you feel drained and depleted.
- You are worth actively investing time and energy into your healing.
- Tapping into your authentic feelings and acting on them can be made easier through journaling, meditation, or working with a healer, coach or therapist.
- Intentionally prioritize your joy.
- It is okay to say "no."
- It is not your responsibility to rescue others from the decisions that they make for themselves.
- We are active participants in our own healing.

The Call to Self-Soothe and Healing Codependency

What happens when people open their hearts?
They get better.
—Haruki Murakami

Identifying the Symptoms

For codependents, we may be able to point to a system, person, or parent and place some blame. While this may be a true part of our story, we must take our power back from living in a blame-state. Abiding in victimhood impedes our progress forward, and we do ourselves a disservice in that role. While a system or person may have wounded, it is now our responsibility to heal ourselves.

Our feelings are our guidance system in our healing. If we have been taught to not trust our feelings or to suppress them, it

1

may take a concerted effort to build up the muscle of listening to our intuitive guidance system.

Our wounds let their presence be known in the form of triggers. Triggers are opportunities to see our value reflected back to us, or to see a part of ourselves in need of attention and *healing*. Triggers can indicate where our boundaries are and, through our feelings, we can begin heading towards our expansion and growth by listening to what our triggers are trying to say. They can be opportunities to make a shift.

If we don't address our childhood wounds, they can show up later. Unmet needs from our childhood can become a subliminal expectation for our partners to fulfill. Our past wounding can build a shaky foundation for future love.

Until healed, our hurting inner child has the capacity to call some important shots. Traumatic residue produces perceived inadequacies that creep into our adult relationships. This residue can impact our conversations around salaries, the formation of friendships, and investments in relationships. It can impact our ability to take our bodies, health, time, or resources seriously. Our wounds are like ticking time bombs awaiting an emotional trigger to show us they have been present but dormant.

Healing Our Inner Child

Self-soothing is giving attention, nurturing, and validation to the emotions our wounds bring to light. The deeper healing work begins when we identify the roots of our self-abandonment. This can begin by honestly identifying emotions we may have long buried. We use reflections in future chapters to identify any stubbornly lodged belief systems that may need overturning.

Making soul-level, or genuine, self-care a priority is an important part of the process. Developing a rhythm for listening to our feelings and intuition is important for steering ourselves into a new way of showing up in our lives. This inner listening enables us to be more discerning in our existing and future relationships. Finally, finding ways to generate more joy and intentionally incorporating them as you process and digest all that may come to light will be balancing and supportive for this healing process.

In the process of nurturing and self-soothing, we are able to further discover our most authentic selves. We can begin to be capable of meaningfully giving, while still self-honoring in the process. Through healing these suppressed knots, we can begin to move beyond the silent captors of our self-limitations.

As adults, we acknowledge the wounded child recognizing that our beliefs surrounding not being enough are self-limiting. As we release the bondage of codependency or people-pleasing and begin aligning more with our own needs, we gradually balance the scales of giving and receiving. We can become the protagonist in our own story, again.

Passively waiting on time to heal our wounds is a form of self-sabotage. Putting in the work of *feeling* through the past and consciously adopting new patterns leads to new ways of moving in our lives. Self-awareness and the potential for cultivating a deeper sense of self-compassion can be birthed from going inward and bravely doing the work. From there, we can stop clinging or searching externally for the validation that we have been looking for inside of ourselves all along. This validation is not external in the form of an individual who provides that inner foundational self-love and it is from this healing place that we give love that is more genuine.

Self-soothing is the re-parenting of your inner child and recognizing that the first person who needs to give to you is you. As you begin fostering this care or acceptance, you will open up into a whole new way of being in your relationships (which may feel awkward, at first). As you adopt new ways of existing and moving, standing up for yourself, taking up more space, or saying "no," it likely will feel foreign or lonely. You might hold space for yourself differently and begin accommodating different standards. With this process may come a newfound understanding of your value and what you offer, and the recognition that settling for less than is reducing yourself and keeping yourself small.

Dealing with Perfectionism

Before we step into our worthiness, we may establish an unhealthy interconnectedness between our performance and our self-worth. There can be an unspoken performance-based contract we reserve with ourselves that if we do more for our partner, put in more hours at work, or just achieve more that these efforts will boomerang back greater acceptance to us. The core issue in performance-based worthiness lies in not fully accepting ourselves.

It is not in our doing that defines our worthiness. It is in the self-knowing and self-accepting that we are worthy. Until then, we may seek it externally in the form of partners, jobs, or peers. Our worthiness wounds can permeate decisions from the investment of our time, to how we respond to criticism, to the type of partnership we are seeking, to how we treat our bodies.

Feeling like you are enough is not found in working harder, checking a box, or achieving more. It is not found in jumping through hoops to prove your worth to others, and ultimately trying to prove your worthiness to yourself. The lesson is in releasing control from a place of knowing that you are already enough. The personal empowerment and self-love lesson involves not working to seek approval or validation *outside* of yourself. You have been enough all along.

By embracing our flaws and integrating them via self-acceptance, the acceptance of our humanness becomes our new superpower. Our sense of personal power becomes partly rooted in our comfort level with our own imperfections. Take time for healing and rebuilding. Enjoy investing in and cultivating more compassion for yourself.

In nonlinear order and, repeatedly, healing codependency is a step-by-step process of ...

- Recognizing that we have given away too much of our personal power
- Recognizing we have unnecessarily taken on the personal responsibilities of others
- Loving yourself harder
- Redirecting our viewfinder towards ourselves and taking up space
- Noticing any self-sabotaging tendencies moving forward
- Forgiving ourselves
- Forgiving others
- Healing the original wound or trauma bond

Trauma-Bonded Relationships and Childhood Wounds

> Your willingness to look at your darkness is what
> empowers you to change.
> —Iyanla Vanzant

More than two-thirds of American children experience some type of childhood trauma.[1] When we put in the work of healing childhood wounds, we may notice that some current upsets can be traced back to an original root from our past. Trauma covers a broad range, including neglect or losing a loved one too early. Not always defined by a looming capital "T," it also houses the lowercase "t" traumas. These are still trauma to feel and heal.

Inner-child healing after trauma is necessary for moving forward, as residual feelings manage to stealthily find their way into adulthood. Leading trauma-based researcher Bessel van der Kolk MD writes in his work, *The Body Keeps the Score,* that "traumatized people have a tendency to superimpose their trauma on everything around them..."[2] Van der Kolk also writes that "for real change to take place, the body needs to learn that the danger has passed and to live in the reality of the present."[3]

Healing wounds passed down from our families becomes a spiritual level of care. In our breaking, our beliefs are revealed, and our feelings have the opportunity to be honored and processed. We also have the opportunity to release stuck energy we have been holding onto and suppressing. Part of our process of moving forward is becoming honest with ourselves about these feelings, and how they have impacted our mind-set. Handed-down brokenness is not our fault to have received, and it becomes our responsibility to tend. Through our processing grief and transmuting our past pain, we can find space to breathe new life into ourselves, as that emotional baggage had been blocking our connection with our authentic self.

When our inner children are left hurting, we can be subconsciously waiting on someone to save us. Breaking this cycle requires taking *agency* and actively working on our healing. Instead of handing over that authority to someone else, we prioritize taking action towards our well-being. Taking responsibility for our healing and any investments where we are kept small is a part of the healing entryway to breaking the cycle.

By looking back at our original wound and metabolizing our past pains, we begin to loosen their grip on our present reality. By identifying any faulty lens through which we have been seeing ourselves, we can habitually work to remove that lens of unworthiness and move forward. Only once we identify the truths of who we are, can we release and separate from a past narrative that has kept us feeling small and unworthy.

Signs Our Inner Child Craves Healing

- Clinging tendencies in relationships
- Inaction towards attainable goals
- Lack of confidence in standing up for oneself or speaking up for one's needs
- Overidentifying with trauma or past wounding
- Clinging onto a victim mentality
- Relationship cycles of being the "fixer" or actively jumping through hoops
- Making others' desires our desires
- Suppressing our voice to keep the peace
- People-pleasing or aligning self-value with outside approval
- Not feeling worthy of goodness, abundance, or love
- Habitual negative self-talk or self-deprecation

Family Ties

As we make the choice to move from an ancestral culture of emotional suppression into one of greater vulnerability, we are setting ourselves free. As younger generations dive into self-healing work, we tip the seesaw from emotional contraction towards release and healing.

Generational wounds are real and passed down. Each of us is inherently a unique individual canvas *and* impacted by those before us. Each of our parents arrive imperfect and at the consciousness level they are at in their life. If a parent carries past trauma, this doesn't excuse or belittle any treatment or abuse, but it can offer a window into a larger perspective for those who heal from the cycle.

While quickly rushing to forgiveness might not be realistic, forgiveness is the key to unlocking and freeing ourselves. Forgiveness is not condoning behavior. Once our wounds are felt and processed, this experience can continually guide us to forgive them and ourselves.

But, first, feel the feelings attached to your childhood. Process how circumstances, words, and actions made you feel. Consider working with professional guidance as you spend time with any lingering difficult feelings and learned inherent beliefs. Maybe, these have been carried around like an added appendage. In future chapters, you will be guided along some steps that you can take to strategically remove this appendage.

Trauma-Bonded Relationships and Codependency

When an inner wound needs attention and healing, we can begin to see cycles or patterns in our relationships. A trauma-bonded relationship is where two people echo one another's unmet childhood needs. In these relationships, there can be an unspoken expectation for others to meet these unmet needs. Early childhood trauma can lead to trauma-bonded relationships.

Trauma-bonded relationships are highly codependent. They may look like a partner silencing their feelings and prioritizing another's feelings ahead of their own. From somewhere in their past, the subliminal message may have been that their feelings were not a priority. The underlying message from one or more people may have been "How you feel doesn't matter as much as how your feelings make me feel."

Codependency occurs as the result of a lie we believe about ourselves—that we are not enough, whole, or complete inside of ourselves, and that we have to outsource our inherent worth. Later in adulthood, the codependent is actually looking for acceptance within themselves. In an effort to find it, validation may be sought from others to fulfill past invalidated emotions.

Codependents may see the same pattern with different partners, in an attempt to correct an old narrative. This bondage may be the result of trying to prove and feel they are enough or worthy, and from wanting to prove the past story untrue. The desire to heal the old storyline and feel like "enough" can lead them towards self-destructive behavior, destructive partners, or outsourcing joy to their partners. Trauma-bonded relationships can keep people stuck in painful or abusive relationships.

A trauma-bonded response may be addiction to the pattern of a relationship where acceptance is found by jumping through hoops for their partner, or where there is a pressure to prove that they are enough or worthy. Sometimes, these relationships can also be characterized by catastrophizing. Sometimes, they can stir more intense emotional responses pointing towards lingering past pain in need of healing.

Codependents can place themselves in "giver" roles, accepting a false responsibility for someone else's dilemmas or circumstances. They may be attracted to partners who are "projects" to be healed or fixed. For codependents, red flags may be ignored in the hope that perceived potential will become reality. Codependents overgive in all types of ways—through their resources, energy, being overly available or hyper problem-solving for others. To protect others or meet their needs, codependents often minimize the impact others have on them.

Partners for trauma-bonded relationships do not have to be romantic. This can show up as people-pleasing, or fawning, and can exist in professional relationships and family dynamics, as well as friendships.

As current wounds from trauma-bonded relationships can make fresh childhood wounds, we are presented with the opportunity to heal the original wound.

Worthiness Wounds

Worthiness wounds can lead to self-abandonment, self-sabotage, or accepting unavailable partners. Coping mechanisms for unhealed childhood wounds can look like the fear of slowing down or the fear of vulnerable connection. A lack of worthiness can present itself as love addiction and love avoidance. Worthiness wounds can lead someone to avoid their feelings through impulsivity, such as consuming food, substances, alcohol, or projects just to keep moving.

Self-abandonment compromises our health in more obvious ways. Self-abandonment can catch up via debt, enduring pain in relationships, or latching onto careers with abusive employers.

The presence of codependency or worthiness wounds can attract narcissistic or abusive partners.

Narcissistic Partners

In order to not repeat the cycle with a narcissist, educating yourself as a victim of emotional abuse is important. Numerous resources are available for help identifying narcissistic partners, but here we place that energy and focus back onto *you* and your movement forward. Focusing on you again after toxic relationships is a key component for growth out of that cycle. Being attached to seeking justice from emotional abuse or ruminating on the pain from abusive partners can be a diversion from jumpstarting your own healing process. Focusing on your growth and healing, while not repeating the cycle, is vital.

Simply leaving codependent relationships or relationships with narcissistic partners does not heal the root cause of them or codependency. Simply leaving without healing carries a risk of repeating the cycle. After these relationships, healing requires seeing past partners clearly *and* seeing your role in these relationships. Moving forward, this self-reflection is part of your own evolution, which leaves you in a healthier state to better discern future partners. A healing component of this process is also accepting that someone's behavior towards you is not a reflection of what you truly deserve. An honest self-assessment could be an opportunity to make a lasting change in how you exist in your relationships, better discern a future partner, and an overhaul for how you care for yourself.

It is hugely beneficial to ramp up self-care practices, in general, following any unhealthy relationship. These partnerships usually take a toll on your mental, emotional and physical health. Often, physical symptoms or chronic fatigue present themselves.

After experiencing deception or loss in relationships, it can feel like it is not safe to give and/or take. It is safe, however, for you to love. If you find yourself healing from one of these relationships, take heart. Not everyone is your past. You are safe to love and to be loved. Keep this as a mantra.

What Waking Up Looks Like

Healing requires identifying that the current cycles of codependency and joy outsourcing are not working. Instead of rescuing a partner, breaking the cycle looks like rescuing ourselves. Healing codependency is redirecting the viewfinder onto ourselves. It is finding alignment between identifying and standing up for our own needs. In addition to releasing abusive partners, it can look like reclaiming agency over our lives. It is recognizing that it is not selfish to take care of ourselves.

Healing can begin by not treating yourself how someone else's actions made you feel. It can look like awakening to the recognition that you've been living softly in your relationships and not speaking up. Eventually, it can result in learning to seek closure within yourself and moving forward.

A part of healing codependency is aligning with real responsibilities and not taking on the responsibilities of others. It involves working on reversing the belief that it is your job to fix someone else, and learning how to recognize where you may have taken on too much responsibility for others. It is releasing people-pleasing tendencies and taking up space. As you learn to listen to your needs and act on them, you avoid reaching the point of overgiving or feeling resentful.

Healing from codependency and people-pleasing may look like greater communication and showing up more for yourself. It is speaking up when the other person may not like it. It is standing your ground for your truth and your heart. Healing inner wounds begins with identifying what false belief has been keeping you down for the sake of freeing yourself from it.

When codependents actively heal their inner children, they work on self-soothing, acknowledging their feelings, taking up space and, finally, accepting responsibility for loving *themselves*. A healing relationship for a recovering people-pleaser looks like a relationship with healthy give-and-take, and being open to *receiving* love. Continually forgive yourself if you self-abandoned by compromising your needs.

Next Steps: Moving Forward and Actively Healing

At some point, we wake up to the choice of staying where we are or moving forward. We drop the limitations of a self-defeating mind-set that have been holding us back, and we crave moving forward. By letting go of the blaming of anyone or anything else, we get to stand tall and take back our power.

Time, alone, does not heal trauma. *Actively* investing in our healing and being kind to ourselves along that journey is the healing choice. Through actively working on ourselves, we have unique opportunities to cleanse and move through our own stuckness. We then can practice both acceptance and release. We are giving back to ourselves love, reflecting back to our inner child that "you are seen and heard and valued," which might not have been felt in our early years. In this reflection, we can begin to break cycles of codependency or people-pleasing. Once that original wound is addressed and heard, we show up differently in the world. A new life is available once we work on our internal blockages.

We now have the opportunity to restructure the way we give and receive love from others. We have the chance to form boundaries in place of the loosely dotted lines that we may have allowed to be easily stepped over in our past. Standing up for ourselves can feel lonely. In the process of recalibrating our value, the pendulum swings away from being seen as small in relationships and in our lives, and brings balance back for ourselves. This is an abandonment of the old way of being where it could have benefitted others for us to remain small. In the process of standing up differently in relationships, others likely may shift in or out of your life. We discuss this more and about standing in your truth in the next chapter.

Authenticity and
Your Inner Circle

The root of compassion is compassion for oneself.
—Pema Chödrön

Healing codependency and worthiness wounding requires time spent alone. Try to cultivate a greater capacity to sit alone with yourself and the comfort found there. You may want to create a space to intentionally be present, mindful, and alone. Eventually, this area or nook can become a cornerstone in your day, as you are creating a practice of going within.

In this healing process, we may find that we require taking our energy and become necessarily and intentionally stubborn with it. It is from this place of holding compassion for ourselves that we can begin to give to others without underlying codependency or losing ourselves in the process. We need to build ourselves whole in order to invest back into others in more healthy ways. Through this experience, you can come through the other side as a more genuine expression of YOU moving in the world.

Cocooning to Heal

As you create new strategies for making healthy changes and new ways of being, your vulnerability and sensitivity meter can run high. Be gentle with yourself and rest, or cocoon, when you need it. If you're highly sensitive to others and their energy, pulling back will be most beneficial for you.

Your relationship dynamics may shift as you pull back and work to recalibrate and heal yourself. Try to let go of any desire to prove anything or pretend to be a superhero, as you take a necessary social slumber. In this freedom from the projections of others, you will likely find it easier to explore. In quiet solitude, you have the chance to cultivate inner comfort and strength. You can show nurturing to yourself, and your inner child, as you complete the reflections in the following chapter and take time out for mindfulness practices alone. In releasing people-pleasing while you focus on and heal yourself, try to release control over the outcome of relationships or situations, and open your heart to yourself.

Be discerning to who you decide to bring your breakthroughs. Sometimes, even those who love you will bring their doubts into the conversation or their fear of change. When we are transforming, our relationships are bound to shift. You are "getting your sea legs" as you align with new truths and make decisions from a newly empowered place. The type of support you might need on your healing journey will not need you to conform to a certain way for them or their comfort. This support type will not be triggered by your suffering into a reliving of their past wounds. In this dynamic, you have the freedom to feel how you are feeling and take up space if you need to do so.

The investment of your energy and the people you surround yourself with matter, and is particularly true in times of transformation and healing. Staying stuck and small for the comfort of others is not to your benefit. Honor your growth. Keep moving and keep growing.

Lessons of Self-Acceptance from Trauma-Bonded Relationships

As touched on in the previous chapter, some relationships reflect back to us our own insecurities and wounds left unhealed. They provide us with insight into where we need to release old patterns and ways of being in our relationships. Through these relationships, we learn where we haven't fully accepted ourselves. Trauma-bonded relationships can help us to see these self-imposed chains and point us back to the original root cause. This awareness and our investment in healing loosens these chains. Such relationships reveal a hidden sense of unworthiness for us to address.

Through these relationship types, we are provided with the opportunity to transmute that pain into our evolution. After we surrender, we can find that these relationships teach us lessons and lead to our soul growth. They allow us the blatant choice to say no to an old way of being, and to embrace a new way of investing in ourselves. Seeing these ignored or repressed parts of ourselves affords us the opportunity to springboard towards personal healing and deeper empathy. In his book on empathy, *The War for Kindness,* Jamil Zaki writes on trauma victims:

[v]ictims' are often stereotyped as weakened by trauma, but many emerge stronger and more fulfilled. "Post-traumatic growth"—including greater spirituality, stronger relationships, and a renewed sense of purpose—is almost as common as PTSD. Survivors who feel a deepened empathy and act on it are most likely to report post-traumatic growth.

By recalibrating our sense of worth and valuing our time, energy, and effort differently, we can spring forward on our journey with greater connectivity to others and a greater sense of purpose.

Notes on Just "Vibing Higher"

In all times, focusing on gratitude and what is positive is nourishing. But, in healing, authentically accepting harder truths and feeling painful emotions is a part of the process of releasing our stuck pain. Sometimes, a chorus of "just be happy" can deny the experience of those with trauma in need of healing. It is important that the vibing-higher message is not meant to bypass or overlook the expense of someone processing pain or stuck emotions. True healing is messier than a "just smile" message. If you find yourself surrounded by this opinion of vibing higher, deny the pressure to *be* for others and accept that it does not deny any intense emotions that need working through from the past.

Listening to Your Inner Guidance

In cultivating our inner relationship, we are opening up to the opportunity to learn how to listen to our own inner guidance. Through practices of mind-body connection, we can develop greater trust in our feelings. We can draw awareness back into our body – here and now. We start noticing when something is not sitting right in our body, sometimes via tension.

Trauma or wounding can keep us feeling disconnected from our inner guidance system. Your body's inner guidance may have been trying to warn you in the past by using red flags. By increasing time spent going inward and through mindfulness, we can learn to listen and trust our inner guidance. We may begin or continue cultivating a spiritual practice from this process. As we build this muscle of surrender, we can listen and respond self-lovingly to future red flags by using our voices and boundaries. Eventually, we can continue honoring ourselves by not dismissing or figuratively sweeping our emotions under the rug any longer.

Say What You Mean, Mean What You Say

A high cost is associated with emotional toughness or rejecting ourselves by not honoring our voice. Dismissing and attempting to develop a thick emotional skin translates into a closed heart and stuck physical energy in the body. This high expense can block the flow of love coming in or going out. If we don't speak it, we keep it stored in and locked away.

Taking the time out to identify and sticking to your feelings in your relationships through your words pulls back the petals from closing up. Honor your voice. Your feelings are your true north.

Hey, Ladies!

As you heal and transform, it's natural to grieve your old conditioned self. You might mourn parts of your old self as you change for the healthier. You are removing the blinders and, perhaps, some tendencies are coming out to indicate to you what to heal.

As women, pulling back to heal will likely deny conditioning that it is a part of your purpose to be what other people need you to be for them. I once listened to a lecture on enneagram testing, a personality test with nine types or ways of viewing ourselves in the world. A leader on this topic explained that if you are a woman, due to societal conditioning, your test results may be a two. A two is coined "the giver." Your actual type, however, may be different. Out of all nine types, most women could be reduced to one single test result, and it was attributed to conditioning. Once a dynamic is set up that reinforces our roles to us, we can begin to see this dynamic play out repeatedly in life.

Whether or not we are conscious of any potentially self-limiting beliefs, the beliefs we hold about ourselves act as a rudder guiding our ship. Through the work of reflections, affirmations, and emotional freedom technique lies the invitation to draw your attention back to the beliefs that impact our relationship with ourselves and with others.

Breaking the Cycle Looks Like Recognizing

- You can always speak up for yourself and what you will not tolerate.
- Sometimes, you have to walk away.
- Sometimes, the best move is walking away.
- You have always been enough to take up space and stand your ground.
- When people show you who they are, release your expectations of them.

Inner Child Reflections and Mindset Healing

If I'm searching for my spirituality
Passionately, I must begin with me.
—Jill Scott

Writing has been a saving grace and a safe space for me. For as long as I can remember, I have kept some form of a journal, and have written in times when I have felt like it or not. Writing seems to find a way of coaxing out truths that have been left unrecognized within.

Discovering these truths by reflecting on paper can help us to process all that we are, and to reveal any lies that we have been holding onto. Writing out our emotions can be an easier way to begin drawing our truths up to the surface. When it's tough to speak it or admit it to ourselves, writing it out can be a gateway to bringing it out into the open. Through this practice, we can identify any negative self-talk, recognize neglected feelings and, ultimately, cultivate greater self-acceptance.

Freestyle Reflecting

Simply, begin writing out your feelings. Allot yourself the time to do this. You might want to do this when your head is the most clear, and when you will be the least distracted (like the early morning). Sometimes, creating more structure around this time, such as setting an amount of time or an amount you will reflect or write, can be the best method for continually getting it done. You might want to try a method of continually writing where you do not stop to judge or edit. Simply allow the pen to continue moving across the page. If you wish to use it, there is a *notes* section for you at the end of this book.

When in doubt, speak from the vantage point of your own feelings. If you feel stuck, you can start really simply with "I felt … when … happened or was said" or "I felt hurt/angry/let down when … ".

Guided Reflections

To help with this process, use the prompts below. You might want to break these up into several days.

- Imagine a time when you felt triggered in the recent past. Sit with the emotions from that for a moment. Reflect by writing on it, noting that you might find more than one answer.

- What is it about this triggering situation that actually bothered me?

- In this triggering instance, when have I felt this emotion further back in my past?

- In the past, when did I abandon my needs for others? (Explore different times and circumstances and how these left you feeling.)

- Growing up, who validated my emotional experiences?

- Growing up, who carved out space for me to be me? How did they do this? How did this feel?

- How have I looked after an immediate need for myself recently? (After identifying one, reflect on a few instances)

- How have I let myself receive love? (Reflect on a few instances.)

- What are my feelings surrounding worthiness and feeling worthy of receiving love from others?

- Recently, how have I shown myself that I care for myself? (Reflect on a few instances).

- How do I routinely show myself that I care for myself? What practices already exist in my routine to do this?

- How have I shown love and shown another's worthiness to receive love?

- How have I been taught to receive love? How has the dynamic been in terms of being the giver or the provider of love? How has this dynamic played out in other partnerships and relationships in my life?

Affirmation of Your Vision

For one who has conquered the mind, the Supersoul is
already reached, for he has attained tranquility. To such
a man happiness and distress, heat and cold, honor and
dishonor are all the same.
— *Bhagavad-gita* 6.7

When I began working with affirmations, it felt simultaneously necessary and foreign. Sometimes, I wouldn't feel anything attached with what I was saying, but occasionally, I would feel an empowering jolt from a particular affirmation. I believe these take time. But, saying them is a tool for when when we are going through transformational periods and needing to reconnect with our inner strength and reclaim our courage.

Due to our brain's built-in negativity bias, negative events have more significant impact than positive ones. We recall traumatic events more vividly than positive events, and we tend to fixate on criticism amidst an otherwise glowing review or positive experience.

As we perform new habits, including affirmative self-talk and positive mind-set work, we strengthen neural pathways linked to positive emotional responses. When we make repeated, positive changes, the repeated firing of neurotransmitters becomes stronger and this new pathway can become our new normal. Over time, creating a practice around retraining our thought loops and working against our inherent negativity bias can relieve the grasp of any tired and untrue story we may be telling ourselves. Thankfully, we can change our existing thought tendencies and breathe hope and peace into our story, here and now.

A growing amount of research shows that our thought patterns and emotions have effects on our physical body and can even influence the onset of numerous illnesses, including arthritis and cancer.[4] Similarly, studies on the impact of sound on bloodwork indicate that disturbing sounds produced pathological changes in the blood.[5]

Dr. Masaru Emoto is known for his experiments showing the impacts of sounds and words on the composition of water crystals. Emoto published a bestselling book with pictures of the microscopic patterns found in natural water crystals from his experiments. His pictures revealed that when harsh sounds were played over water, the composition of the crystals appeared dull and formless. When melodious sounds were presented, the crystals formed intricate and discernable configurations. Dr. Emoto's water crystal findings revealed the visual effects of specific environments and messages on the universal element of water.

Emoto's experiments suggest that the words we tell others and ourselves may have an impact on our bodies, which are made up of around 70 percent water.[6]

After many years, Emoto concluded and believed that "positive thinking will strengthen your immune system and help to set you moving towards recovery—a fact that the medical community is starting to wake up to."[7]

Writing Affirmations

The power of our speech—saying out loud life-affirming statements—carries a powerful movement of energy with it. By stating these affirmations out loud, we detach from our old outlooks and work on releasing mind-sets based in fear and anxiety. Through the work of affirmations, we are actively choosing love.

To start, begin envisioning your ideal self and health at a specific number of years in the future.

- In your mind's eye, what do you see?
- Where do you see yourself?
- What feelings do you have when you picture your future self?
- What emotions do you allow in, and what would you like to receive?
- Are you with anyone? If so, who?
- What do you look like?

Map out what life looks and feels like in your vision. If you are having trouble answering or do not have clarity surrounding this picture, try taking a longer moment to envision it. You might find meditating on this or writing about it is helpful to solidify it.

Once you have created this vision in your mind, move on to creating affirmations. "I am" is a good starting place for writing affirmations. You can write these in the present tense and focus on the positive (rather than incorporating how you *don't* want to feel). If an affirmation feels inauthentic for you, choose an affirmation that resonates instead. Only you know what resonates for you.

The basis for your affirmations may also be the reversal of any self-limiting beliefs that you hold.

This may feel a little odd at first. Say them out loud to yourself (maybe, while even looking at yourself). Like your writing and reflections work, try to make these a practice.

Examples include:

- I am enough.
- I am worthy.
- I am finding freedom from an old story.
- I am embracing my transformation.
- I am courageous.
- I am finding freedom from self-sabotaging beliefs.
- I am aligning with my authentic self.
- I am letting go of self-imposed limitations.
- I am continually showing up for myself.
- I show myself grace and love.
- I allow grace and love to enter.
- I am being made whole.

You can also use statements that do not start with "I."

Examples of these may include:

- Peace resides in me.
- Love flows within me.
- Clarity moves through me.

As growing amounts of mind-body research show that our thoughts contribute to our overall health, it begs us to take a closer look at our thoughts and manage them. As Dr. Masaru Emoto wrote, "When your heart is open to possibilities, you start to notice small things that can lead to enormous discoveries."[8]

Releasing with Emotional Freedom Technique

If you change the way you look at things,
the things you look at change.
—Wayne Dyer

What the mind forgets, the body stores away. Emotional Freedom Technique, also referred to as EFT or "tapping," is the literal tapping with one or several fingers on specific meridian points of the upper body combined with spoken words. It provides a natural way to soothe our nervous system and release stuck energy. Emotional Freedom Technique targets our subconscious beliefs or conscious fears. As it works with points of higher energetic concentration throughout the body, EFT can be a way to release self-sabotaging beliefs and obstacles.

This work can reveal the thoughts that we didn't know we had been storing away in our bodies. In studies, it has been shown to lower cortisol levels, help manage emotional eating, and produce positive outcomes for coping with trauma.[9],[10] EFT can be geared towards a specific focus, such as releasing fear and anxiety.

To be most effective, the statements you use need to resonate with you. In this chapter, a sample script is provided for you to use. This script is geared towards releasing unworthiness and cultivating greater self-acceptance. You might choose to use this script or adopt it as a framework, editing it with statements that resonate with you.

To form your script, speak from your feelings and start the process by identifying any limiting beliefs. Any blockages or fears surrounding money, relationships, personal value, and worthiness are all worthy of exploring. The next step of this process is then identifying the affirmative. For each self-limiting statement, identify how you would like to feel, stating the new compassionate affirmation. By moving into these new affirmations, we honor these new beliefs about ourselves and our situation.

Some general guidelines:

- Switch points with each sentence or two.
- The tapping can be done at a medium pace on each point.
- Speak each line aloud.
- Think and feel each message.
- Try to release any judgment of yourself or of the process.
- You may want to use a rating scale before and after, such as rating anxiety level on a scale of 1-10.

In the following illustration, you'll find the points to literally "tap" on as you say these words out loud to yourself. You might want to do this in the mirror. The points to connect (which align with meridians, or energetic points) include the top of head, eyebrow, side of the eye, under the eye, under the nose, chin, collarbone, the "karate chop" part of the hand, and under the arm.

You might want to prep by taking a few deep breaths, or by performing a calming breathwork exercise on your own.

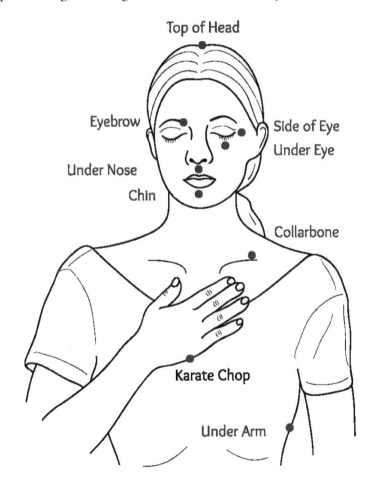

EFT Tapping Points

EFT Script for Self-Acceptance and Releasing Unworthiness

- I am freeing myself from any lingering feelings of shame or unworthiness.
- I believe good things come from letting go.
- It is not easy to let go.
- I believe healing comes from release.
- Until now, I have been scared of change and felt stuck.
- Accepting my own wholeness has been scary.
- I have felt unworthy of stepping into my own completeness.
- I have felt unworthy of _____.
- I have felt unworthy because of _____.
- In the past, I have hid my pain by self-abandoning.
- I hid my pain by ignoring my truth.
- Letting go of unworthiness is something I am accepting.
- I believe that breaking old patterns is possible.
- I know releasing this old way of being is best for me.
- I can let go of feeling unworthy.
- I am letting go of any area of my life where I have denied myself.
- I am letting go of not accepting my worthiness.
- I am stepping out of past hurtful patterns.
- I am releasing an old way of being in my life.
- I know that I am worthy.
- I accept that I am enough.
- I feel free when I accept that I am enough.
- I am releasing my fear surrounding these feelings.
- I am releasing fear.
- My body is no longer storing these feelings. I release them.
- I forgive myself for abandoning and overlooking my inherent value.
- I am worthy of feeling free.

- I am already enough.
- I am love.
- Letting go feels good and new.
- I choose to be more courageous.
- As I show myself grace, I feel better.
- I am finding freedom as I accept my worthiness of it.
- I am growing in love for myself.
- I am growing in love for others.
- I release that which does not serve my highest good.

The Mind-Body Connection and Meditation

These three processes—*being* with whatever arises, *working*
with the tendencies of mind to transform them, and *taking*
refuge in the ground of being—are the essential practices
of the path of awakening.
—Rick Hanson

I believe my body had been storing away what my mind and
heart were not fully ready to process. As grief boiled to the
surface, I coped by pushing myself harder in other avenues
and aspects of life. I started physically running to distract myself
and find release. I poured more of my efforts into my work.
Eventually, I began to experience multiple inflammation-related
symptoms and feel burnt out.

Instead of pausing to reconnect and listen to what my body and
feelings were trying to say, I pushed harder against the emotional
tide. Once I surrendered and allowed what was pushed down

come to the surface, I felt these emotional floodgates fling open. I went through the persistent release of old pain, allowing the truth to infiltrate my wounds and letting light propel me forward.

The main spiritual practices in the world are based on a foundational premise that we are spiritual beings having a physical experience. A shared belief is that we are more than our bodies, or our emotional states, and that our souls are separate from and temporarily connected to our bodies.

Healing is the intentional work of focusing on all aspects of ourselves — our physical, emotional, mental and spiritual health. In previous chapters, we targeted our belief systems and surrendering to the process of rewriting our story. We began to target the movement of energy through the body, as trauma and emotions stay nestled inside our physical body. In this chapter, we explore the integration of the body and mind and some of the research behind that connectivity.

Mindfulness Research

Increasing amounts of research indicate a link between mindfulness practices and the calming of the central nervous system.[11] As touched on in the discussion on EFT, the physical manifestation of stress in the body is connected with our thoughts, and thought-looping hurtful narratives can lodge pain in the body stunting our ability to move forward.

The Limbic system is the brain's structural system for increasing emotional conscious awareness and houses our amygdala. The amygdala is considered to be the storage center for emotional trauma and holds memories connected with fear and anxiety.[12] It is also a key part of the brain for processing emotions like fear and anxiety throughout the body.[13] When a threat is perceived, not only is the amygdala activated, but the firing up of the sympathetic nervous system, our body's fight-or-flight response, occurs. This is our body's high-alert alarm and survival mechanism. Physical symptoms like upper-body tension and an increased heart rate are manifestations of perceived threats from our intrinsic fight-or-flight response. In addition to feelings of anxiety, the sympathetic nervous system is linked with high cortisol levels, a reduction in serotonin production, increased blood pressure, and an increased heart rate.

This activation of the parasympathetic nervous system calms and counters the stress response from the sympathetic nervous system. Research shows that practicing mindful awareness can activate the parasympathetic nervous system, calming our fight-or-flight response and naturally helping us manage our stress.[14] It sends calming messaging throughout the body that "all is well."

The parasympathetic nervous system activates in response to specific intentional breathing and can reduce the heart rate, promoting feelings of calm and safety. Research shows that mindful awareness can lead to decreased levels of anxiety and anger, and stimulate parts of the brain linked to joy and contentment.[15,16,17] Mindfulness practice has also been linked to easing chronic pain and improving sleep.[18,19]

Dr. Bessel Van der Kolk states, "...mindfulness practice is the cornerstone for recovery from trauma." Our emotional stuckness and current fears resulting from early trauma can be loosened by engaging in intentional mindfulness practices. Engaging in mind-body activity, or mindfulness, is a way we can proactively manage our anxiety and stress and begin to set ourselves free. Amy Weintraub writes in *Yoga Skills for Therapists,*

> [s]omething happens in our lives and we aren't ready or able to process it, to let the emotion move through. Even when memory is repressed, the body remembers. The stored impressions from past actions can prevent us from experiencing life without preconceived limits.[20]

Yoga

Yoga nidra, hatha yoga, and somatic psychology all share beliefs around actively releasing bound pain that has been lodged in the body for improved health. Research has shown positive results for increasing gamma-Aminobutyric Acid (GABA) levels linked to physical yoga practice, or *asana*. When these levels are low, they can contribute to anxiety and depression.[21] In other studies, yoga has also been shown to reduce anxiety and improve mood and well-being.[22]

While the physical practice of yoga promotes mind-body connection, it is larger than just this practice. The practice of yoga also includes breathing practices (pranayama), and meditation (dhiyana), as well as chanting. Chanting is typically done in the forms of mantra, Japa, or kirtan. The larger practice of yoga is intended and studied as a connection of the mind, body, and spirit, with the ultimate goal of reaching Samadhi, or a completely liberated state. Through remaining present, an emphasis on not worrying about the future or living in the past, greater connection is sought and elevation of ourselves through yoga or "yoking" with a spiritual source/God.

As mentioned earlier, practicing breathwork, or conscious breathing practice, can activate the parasympathetic nervous system, calming our fight-or-flight response and, naturally, reducing our stress.

In times of uncertainty or stress, connecting with our breath is an especially helpful practice. In yogic teachings, the breath allows for prana, or the life force, to enter the body and draw in necessary restoration and life. The inhalation or drawing in of prana is key for sustained vitality, and impacts the mental, emotional, and physical body. Constricted breaths result in perceived stress by the body. The mind does not receive as much oxygen, thus, our muscles constrict and our fascia is dried.

Feeding the Soul Through Meditation and Spiritual Practice

We are always ruminating, focusing our mental energy somewhere. As the saying goes, "energy flows where attention goes."

Meditation is the practice of growing in awareness, being present in the body and in the now. It can simply look like gaining conscious awareness of the thoughts that pass through our mind, steering our course. Meditation helps us remain present in the now, without sitting in the past or fast-forwarding to the future. Gaining conscious awareness can help us better control our thought patterns. Meditation can also be a spiritual practice.

Meditation can involve drawing our focus to one thing, phrase, or our breath. Intentions for meditation may include the reduction of stress, gaining presence, connecting with oneself or connecting with a higher source. Scientifically, it has been shown to increase neurological activity in the parts of the brain associated with joy, and believed to help combat anxiety, depression, and physical pain symptoms in the body.[23] Meditation may be centered around one focal point, our breath, a mantra, a theme like compassion, or on various parts of the body.

In ancient Hindu practice, meditation can include a mantra mediation and/or incorporating the use of a physical object like a set of beads in Japa mediation. Japa meditation involves the repetition of a mantra. This use of a physical symbol in the form of a set of beads, as in Japa, and the practice of using mantra has been scientifically shown to calm the central nervous system.[24]

Mantras have been used in spiritual practice for thousands of years across multiple continents. Broken down, the word *mantra* is "Ma," meaning mind, and "tra," meaning that which frees or sets you free from the mind. The use of sound can encourage the focus back onto our breathing, drawing awareness to how we feel inside of our own body.

Starting a Mindfulness and Meditation Practice

There is no strict rule for performing this practice.

Let yourself sit comfortably with your spine extended (rather than slouching, compressing the vertebrae or your internal organs). If sitting upright is not comfortable for you, try lying comfortably on the floor.

Begin in a space that is free from distractions and by closing your eyes. If you prefer to keep your eyes open, you might try allowing your gaze to be soft. Depending on the time of day or your schedule, setting an alarm may be helpful.

Start noticing how you feel in your body.

Focus your awareness to your breathing. Draw in your next inhale intentionally through the nose, allowing your breath to lift the belly, and hold it for a count of three. Then release the exhale slowly and completely. Repeat this a little deeper for two more rounds.

Spend the next few breath cycles noticing how you feel in your body. Then, without passing judgment, notice your inhale. Next, notice your exhale. Notice its duration and its placement. Begin to draw your awareness to any other physical sensations as they present themselves throughout your practice.

Simply notice what is coming up for you and how you feel. Try to resist any urge to judge what may come up for you as "good" or "bad." Release any judgment of yourself.

Continue to notice your breath and any shifts that may come up for you. Perhaps, you notice the rising, release, or stillness in specific parts of the body as you breathe—noticing the sensations and feelings that present themselves as you ride along your breath.

As you continue, a thought may arise in the mind. Simply acknowledge any passing thoughts and, gently, bring your focus back to your breath. As your mind may choose to move to the past or towards the future, simply notice this happening and bring your awareness back to the sensation of being present, right now. Notice your feelings of being in your body. Begin to draw your awareness back to how you feel in your body.

You don't need to set an end goal for your practice. As you continue, be kind to yourself.

Gratitude

Incorporating gratitude as a part of your regular routine is another practice linked with increasing happiness. Choose a specific time of the day for this practice, and list and reflect on three-to-five things you were specifically grateful for throughout the course of your day. Take a moment to notice how these moments make you feel. I particularly like doing this at the end of my day and when I am in nature.

Incorporating gratitude is a helpful tool for shifting our perspective, pulling us out of any preoccupied worries or mundane concerns. This awareness and gratitude can help us see a bird's-eye view of our lives and the world.

The compassion that can come about from gaining conscious awareness helps us feel humble and, also, taken care of in a larger sense. Through mindfulness practices like meditation, we have the opportunity to expand our awareness and to begin paying attention to our inner-guidance system. A blossoming compassion for ourselves and appreciation for our inner intuitive guidance helps us develop trust in ourselves and open up to a spiritual practice much larger than ourselves.

Chakras and Personal Reflections for Inner-Child Wounds

Remember, the entrance door to
the sanctuary is inside you.
—Rumi

The purpose of this chapter is to look to the yogic wisdom of the chakras as a means of revealing destructive thought patterns and releasing our blockages.

Chakras are referred to in ancient Vedic texts, dating back around 5,000 years. Chakras are points of high energetic concentration affiliated with our physical, mental, emotional, and spiritual being. The chakras act as connecting points for the nadis—the thousands of subtle energetic channels that run throughout the body. In order for energy to move freely in the body, the chakras must be clear.

Each of these seven energetic points align with specific beliefs. These particular areas are believed to be holding onto deep energetic imprints that can stem from our childhood. As Amy Weintraub states on chakras in her book, *Yoga Skills for Therapists*, "...our traumas, losses, environmental factors, and everyday challenges can create disturbances at these centers that contribute to imbalances and disease."[25]

Studying and understanding the chakras brings up questions regarding our ingrained beliefs and authenticity. Our family, specifically any caregivers, impacted our ideologies and ingrained beliefs and this, in turn, can impact these energetic centers. Who we are and how we identify in the world, including our gender and race, impacts the information we metabolize about ourselves from society and can impact these points.

Focusing on the chakras provides a framework for us to focus on old patterns or ways of being that are out of alignment with our true self. Each of the chakras can be in different states, including being open, blocked or closed. When blocked, it is believed that disease can potentially begin to manifest.

Each of the seven chakras have a physical location ranging from the base of the spine up to the crown of the head. They each correlate to specific colors, body parts, elements, and emotions. Also, there are frequencies, mantras, foods, yoga poses, crystals, and scents independently associated with each of the chakras, and that are intended to help free up the energy around these centers. We will focus on ideologies and questioning our inherent beliefs as they identify with each chakra. Doing so can help us identify where imbalances may be occurring, and help us reflect parts of ourselves in need of mending.

As you learn about the chakras, you will likely begin to notice patterns and see how their representations resonate with you. By understanding what each of the chakras represent and their accompanying belief systems, they can be a helpful tool for sharpening our focus, clearing the clutter and assessing beliefs we hold about ourselves. The chakra reflections can gently show what may need attention.

In each of the chakras' outlines, you will find health indicators of stuck energy and open energy. The reflections and affirmations in this chapter are intended to guide you through the belief systems affiliated with each chakra.

As mentioned, the chakras run from the base of the spine to the crown of the head. Moving from the most physically dense to the most ephemeral, the seven chakras are the root, sacral, solar plexus, heart, throat, third eye, and crown. The first three chakras are considered to be the lower chakras, and are more affiliated with the physical body and the senses. Connected by the heart chakra, the top three chakras are more associated with the spiritual and the ephemeral. It is recommended to move from the base chakra upward, rather than move around or focusing intensely on the upper chakras without grounding. For the purpose of healing old patterns and inner-child wounds, the main focus is drawn to the first four chakras.

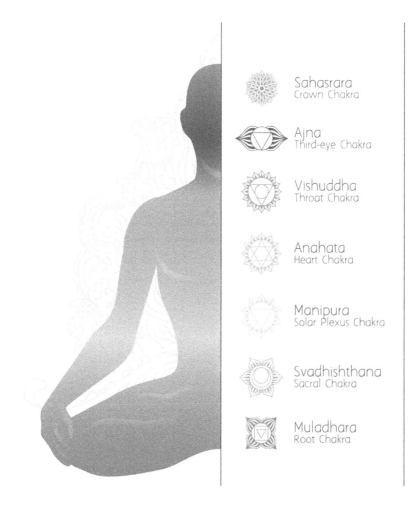

Root Chakra (Muladhara)

The first chakra, the root chakra, is located at the base of the spine and represented by the color red. This chakra represents our sense of security and home, as well as our beliefs affiliated with our most basic necessities. Our feeling of safety within the home is associated with the root chakra. This can also include feeling safe in society and how safe we feel in who we are and how we identify, including our gender, sexual identity, and race.

Feeling a lack of trust is connected with the root chakra. If, especially as a child, we moved often or felt a lack of stability in the home, this can imbalance the root chakra and lead to skepticism in trusting others, or generally feeling ungrounded.

Ways an imbalance can show up include adopting a "live to work" mentality, or defining ourselves by our career. An imbalance may also present itself as a fear of change, such as stuckness in a significant area of life or clinging onto an aspect of our lives too tightly for our stability. If we were deprived of a necessity as a child, it can result in tendencies like hoarding, or an overemphasis on losing our sense of stability. The fear can present itself via compulsive tendencies and an overemphasis on clutching on to what we have from a lack mentality or a fear-based mind-set.

When the root chakra, in particular, is out of balance, it may be the impact of clinging on to a belief system that was handed down from our upbringing. These beliefs, which were subscribed to by our community or our family, can move us out of alignment with our true sense of self and personal stability. As we work on identifying these projected belief systems, we chip away at these stories and unravel their impacts. Physically, an imbalance in the root chakra can present itself as physical pain in the lower part of the body and pelvic issues.

53

Rewriting our story, in alignment with our *personal* truth, and identifying with our truth outside of or despite our upbringing, family dynamic, or societal conditioning, can bring the root into alignment. Healing wounds of enmeshment and finding our independence are freeing themes for the root chakra. By choosing to not suppress our thoughts, actions, and words for the sake of keeping the peace, we can find a sense of grounding and empowerment linked with the root chakra. Grounding in nature, putting our feet in the sand, using our hands working in the earth, and even physical exercise and getting a massage can help balance the root chakra. Creating a habit of practicing affirmations, in general, is balancing for the root chakra.

Root Chakra Reflections

- Growing up, what was my experience like at home?
- Growing up, did I feel safe at home?
- What cultural influences encouraged me in my upbringing?
- Were there any cultural influences to suppress my authentic self in my upbringing?
- What is my current relationship with money?
- Am I scared of money?
- Am I never satisfied or feel like I cannot get enough?
- Do I feel personally secure?
- What is my response to change?
- Am I overly scared of change?

Root Affirmation: I am safe and secure being me.

For further balancing of the root, it is recommended to eat red foods, meditate and ground yourself, and wear or keep red jasper stone.

Sacral Chakra (Svadisthana)

The second chakra, the sacral chakra, is located just below the navel and represented by the color orange. It is connected to our creativity, passion, and sexual energy, and our sense of joy and our expression of it. Like the color orange suggests, it can be fiery, expressive, and energetic.

Sacral chakra imbalances can show up as either extremes of having a low libido or a hyperactive sex drive. An imbalance here may present itself as an overreliance on the validation of others or feeling stuck in our creative pursuits, such as writer's block. Feeling shame, guilt, or suppression surrounding our sexuality or our creative expression is tied to a sacral imbalance. Over time, this imbalance can manifest as a creative passion mentally realized or desired, but suppressed. If our personal expression is controlled by an outside person, family, or group when growing up or presently, it can disrupt the energy in the sacral chakra.

Freely expressing your creative passion, allowing space for joy, and even healing inner-child wounds can free up the energy surrounding the sacral chakra. Moving, playing, dancing, and painting are all activities connected with freeing and clearing sacral energy. When balanced, creative expression is free flowing and we feel like we are in alignment with our passion and purpose.

Sacral Chakra Reflections

- When did I (or have I ever felt) unsafe or inadequate being me?
- When was my vulnerability shot down or used against me?
- Do I believe I need to answer to someone else when it comes to my creative projects or desires?
- What is my honest relationship with sex?

- Am I fearful of physical connection?
- Is my sex drive hyperactive?
- Do I feel free to embrace my unique personal attributes here and now?
- What tangible expressive ways do I connect with and express my creative self?
- Do I feel aligned with my purpose?

Sacral Chakra Affirmation: I am free to express myself creatively. I celebrate my uniqueness.

For further balancing of the sacral chakra, eat orange foods and wear orange. Use carnelian stone.

Solar Plexus—Manipura

The third chakra, the solar plexus, is located just above the naval and represented by the color yellow. The solar plexus is connected with our personal strength and self-esteem, and a healthy self-worth and self-love.

Emotionally, a solar plexus imbalance can show up as a disconnect between what we desire and how we act on our desires for ourselves. Restricting ourselves from stepping into our truth, maintaining a disconnect between what we want and what we do, or not showing up for ourselves in the *doing* in our own lives can imbalance the solar plexus chakra. When out of balance, competitiveness, control issues, and power struggles can present themselves. Feelings of anxiety, nervousness, insecurity, and anger (due to lack of control) are linked to the solar plexus. Physically, the solar plexus is connected with our digestive system, and an imbalance may present itself in the form of indigestion or accumulated stress in this area, as well as feeling tightness in this part of the upper abdomen.

When we are confident in and showing up for ourselves from a place of personal strength, this is correlated with a free and open solar plexus chakra. By cultivating self-love and stepping forward from a place of personal empowerment, the solar plexus chakra energy is free. Releasing the need to control and being confident without being ruled by our ego reflects free-flowing energy in the solar plexus.

Mindfully noticing if tension is being held in this part of the body can be a helpful way to begin working on clearing the solar plexus. Actively combating stress and finding relief through mindfulness and belly breathing are ways of freeing up tightly held energy here. In our relationships, identifying and releasing any controlling tendencies, people-pleasing, or seeking out validation are all important for keeping the solar plexus energy free and clear.

Solar Plexus Reflections

- How am I showing up for my needs and my wants?
- Do I feel confident in expressing my needs and wants?
- Do I feel that I have any power-hungry tendencies?
- Do I believe I may have a low sense of self-worth?
- Where am I sacrificing being me for someone else?
- What can I do to cultivate greater self-love?
- Is there a specific environment where I feel less freedom to be or where I feel a need to control outcomes or others?

Solar Plexus Affirmation: I stand in alignment with my truest self and find inner strength.

For further balancing of the Solar Plexus, eat yellow foods, wear or keep citrine near you, and work with positive affirmations on a regular basis. Perform yoga regularly and try to release stress (particularly as you feel it accumulate in this part of your body).

Heart Chakra—Anahata

The fourth chakra, the heart chakra, is located in the center of the chest and represented by the color green (and sometimes, pink). It is likely the most frequently referenced or commonly-known chakra. One significant element of the heart chakra is that it is the connection point between the three lower chakras, affiliated more with our physical body and our three upper chakras affiliated with our spiritual connection. In this sense, the heart chakra serves as a connector, or a hub. The heart chakra is the seat of unconditional love. It is strongly connected to our sense of self-love and our ability to both give and receive love.

The need for inner-child healing can result in stuck energy around the heart chakra. Early feelings of rejection or abandonment can point towards the need for heart chakra healing. When out of balance, a lack of self-love, codependency, resentment, jealousy, or chronic depression can present themselves. Physically, issues surrounding the heart chakra can show up as physical pain around the chest and, when more chronically closed, can lead to physical heart problems. During times of grieving, this area needs particular attention.

When the energy surrounding the heart chakra is free, this relates to our ability to love ourselves wholly and completely. Opening up to receiving love, relationships characterized by reciprocal love, and having a healthy sense of self-love are all indicators of open energy in the heart chakra.

The heart chakra is delicate. We gently open our hearts by actively healing through cultivating self-love, compassion for others, and tending to our inner child wounds. Heart healing work can involve actively forgiving ourselves and others, healing codependency, practicing letting go, and implementing healthy boundaries.

Heart Chakra Reflections

- What idea might I need to release and let go?
- Who do I need to forgive?
- Is there a relationship I need to release (something from the distant past)?
- Am I open to receiving love from others?
- Do I extend the same compassion to myself that I would give a close friend?
- In what ways do I show myself compassion?
- Do I treat my mind and body kindly?
- Is there healing from my childhood left unaddressed?

Heart Chakra Affirmations: I am worthy of receiving love. I am enough.

For further balancing of the heart chakra: eat and drink green foods, wear and/or keep rose quartz nearby, meditate using a heart-healing frequency (528hz), practice loving-kindness meditations, perform genuine self-care, and work on developing your spiritual practice. Heal inner-child wounds.

Throat Chakra—Vishuddha

The fifth chakra, the throat chakra, is located in the throat and represented by the color blue or turquoise. It is related to our self-expression, communication and creativity.

As mentioned with lower chakra work, personal truth may sometimes lie beneath the layering of formed habits, old stories, and untruthful paradigms that we have picked up from external messages. Like the sacral chakra, our personal expression is tied in to the throat chakra as well.

When the throat chakra is out of balance, we often cannot express ourselves clearly or authentically. Excessive talking, speaking before thinking, fear of speaking our truth, or being deceptive can create disturbances in our throat chakra and are connected to blockages. The physical issues connected with a throat chakra imbalance are thyroid and respiratory problems.

Stuck energy in the throat chakra can be freed by taking up the space to stand in your truth and speaking your truth. This can even relate to our expression through singing. If the motto of "children should be seen and not heard" was a message from our childhood, speaking with a trained therapist or counselor, and having a platform to freely speak is one way to begin reigniting energy in the throat chakra. Activities like singing and chanting as well as simple genuine communication can free up blocked energy surrounding our throat chakra. Embracing our worthiness and speaking authentically clears stuck energy in this chakra.

Throat Chakra Reflections

- Is there something I am afraid to say to others?
- Is there something I am afraid to admit to myself?
- Do I believe it is safe to express myself?
- Do I feel free to take up space?
- Do I extend that freedom to take up space to others in conversation?
- Generally, am I hesitant about expressing myself?
- If I am afraid, why am I holding back?

- If I could put it down in words, how might I express this repressed feeling?
- How does this make me feel?
- Am I afraid to create something that relates to my voice, passion, or purpose?

Throat Chakra Affirmation: I express my truth freely with honesty and integrity.

For further balancing of throat chakra, practice speaking up in any specific circumstances in your life. Practice speaking and writing your truth. Keep sodalite on you or nearby. Sing.

Third Eye Chakra—Ajna

The sixth chakra, the third eye chakra, is located on the forehead between the eyes and represented by the color indigo or deep blue. It governs our intuitive sense and inner clarity.

When we distrust our inner guidance, this lack of clarity is related to a possible imbalance in the third eye chakra. Sometimes, misreading or the inability to see a person or a circumstance clearly can be in an indication of imbalance in the third eye chakra. Headaches, particularly stress headaches, and continual issues relating to sleep can indicate uneasiness here. Physically, this area is connected to our pineal gland and endocrine system. A few indicators of clarity here are having a greater sense of inner awareness, feeling connected to our intuition, and having the ability to perceive others and situations accurately.

For third eye balancing, regularly practicing meditation, painting and keeping a dream journal can assist in freeing up this chakra's energy. Taking time out for breaks free from distractions, particularly digital noise, and focusing on improving our sleep patterns can free up energy in the third eye chakra.

It is important to note that healing of the chakras is all connected and impacts their harmonious functioning. The heart chakra, specifically, is tied into trusting in and harmonious functioning of the third eye chakra.

Third Eye Reflections

- Do I allow myself adequate breaks from the chaos of the world?
- Do I recall my vivid dreams?
- Do I trust my inner knowing?
- Am I distrusting due to an event from the past that may still need attention and healing?
- Do I believe I see others accurately?
- Do I trust my intuition and act on it?

Third Eye Affirmation: I trust my vision and am open to receiving Divine guidance.

For further balancing of third eye chakra, wear or keep labradorite, practice meditation, begin a dream journal, and focus on sleep hygiene.

Crown Chakra—Sahasrara

The seventh chakra, the crown chakra, is located at the very crown of the head and represented by the color violet. Known as the thousand-petaled lotus that opens upward, it is the chakra bringing energy to all the other chakras and related to our spiritual beliefs.

The crown chakra can help us to see from a higher perspective and, ultimately, see glimpses into the connectivity amongst all living beings. It is where a greater sense of knowing is represented. This chakra is linked closely with our spiritual practice and also represents our spiritual relationship with a higher source. Clarity of the crown chakra is linked to a state of pure consciousness and wisdom.

When out of balance, a broad uncertainty or a lack of purpose in life can be felt. When blocked, it may present feelings of disconnectedness or incompleteness. An imbalance may present itself as obsessive worry, feelings of hopelessness, thought loops, or depressive dwelling. Physically, this can present itself as headaches.

Crown Chakra balancing is encouraged through regular meditation, and by cultivating a spiritual practice and spending time in nature.

Crown Chakra Reflections

- In what area of my life am I feeling stuck?
- Where might I be looping in my thoughts?
- Do I show any tendencies towards depression or hopelessness?
- Do I believe things are working out for me outside of my control?
- Do I believe and trust in divine detours and guidance?
- What are my thoughts and feelings surrounding connectivity with all living things?
- Do I currently have a spiritual practice like meditation, connecting in nature, prayer, etc.?

Crown Chakra Affirmation: I move forward in openness and trust. I am ready to receive.

For further balancing of crown chakra, eat purple foods, wear purple, use and wear amethyst, and meditate using crown healing frequencies (963 hertz).

Creating Harmony at Home

We must not cease from exploration
And the end of all our exploring
Will be to arrive where we started
And to know the place for the first time.
—T.S. Eliot

I n this chapter, we will look at daily self-care methods with the
intention of healing and moving forward. Your personal space
has the capacity to be your sanctuary where your most authentic
self is nourished and inspired.

Sleep Hygiene

Sleep hygiene trains our brains for healthy 7–9 hour sleep
cycles in adults. Sleep hygiene is essential for good mental health,
impacting both our mood and memory. Healthy sleep impacts
our central nervous system, as well as our immune, endocrine,
digestive and cardiovascular systems.

As an overall theme, we want to be gentle with ourselves before getting ready to sleep. Creating a relaxing ritual before bed, like using calming essential oils, drinking herbal teas (without caffeine), or using breathing exercises can help create healthy sleep habits. For better sleep hygiene, creating a consistent sleep schedule and setting an earlier bedtime for our electronics is helpful. In today's digitally attached world, these can feel like big shifts.

Because light and sound can stimulate our nervous system, dimming the lights prior to getting ready to sleep and limiting or avoiding reading anything stressful leading up to sleep can set us up for healthier sleep habits. Creating a regular routine of exercise improves the quality of our sleep.

Be Intentional with Routine, Nourishing Self-Care

Drawing from your ideal health vision sketched out from the affirmations section, you can create the routine that best suits the vision you hold for your healthiest self. In this way, you can allow your daily routine to nourish you.

In yogic philosophy, prana-based living foods support and enhance life. From nature, we can receive prana, or life-force abundance, and we receive it from the life-giving foods we eat. Certain foods contain more life-giving energy, and a plant-based diet offers more prana.

Studies show that an alkaline plant-based diet can reduce chronic pain, and even supplementation with alkaline minerals can reduce chronic pain.[26],[27],[28] To support the movement of energy throughout the body and stimulate the lymphatic system, you may consider yoga or consistently incorporating physical activity. This will help to move energy throughout the body.

Developing conscious awareness includes looking into the physical environments where we invest our time and includes our home, our neighborhood, and our work environment. Each environment can contribute to the potential support or decline of our health and well-being.

Harmony in the Home

An environment supporting our wellness and growth is a crucial part of our daily "support system." Look for ways to intentionally incorporate peace at home. Try to listen to and intentionally work on bringing in more of what brings you joy. This could involve incorporating more plants, changing your lighting, taking time to dance, or listening to uplifting music at home. Aesthetically, you might choose to brighten up your space and keep it clutter-free. This space where "less is more" may feel more peaceful and restorative. For those working out of your home, this freeing up of stagnant things and energy may create a place where you feel more free and productive.

Notice the things you are holding onto, particularly, any family heirlooms or sentimental items. Are these items best serving the development and blossoming of where you are headed? Are they attaching you to a past narrative of yourself? Consider eliminating physical things that don't resonate with cultivating joy or with your future vision.

You might also create a space with more intentional listening and watching. Is what you are consuming feeding into where you see yourself or where you desire to head? Are your wind-down habits keeping you bound to where you have been out of alignment with a future vision? You may consider releasing habits and things that don't serve who you are in the process of becoming.

In increasingly digitally leaning times, Dr. Kelly Lambert, an author and behavioral neuroscientist, notes from her research that the use of our hands for activities connects with parts of our brain that lift mood and targets natural depression relief. This is a valuable note: Simply doing activities that require the use of our hands can be healing. Gardening, cleaning, journaling, and painting can all contribute to the strengthening of our neurological connectivity with our sense of well-being and inner happiness.

Harmony in the City

Metropolitan living can result in more a consistent activation of our body's sympathetic nervous system and can repetitively raise our cortisol levels. In addition to working against nature deprivation in these areas, intentional focus on activating the parasympathetic nervous system through mindfulness-based stress-relieving activities can lower cortisol levels and provide a counteracting peace.

Is your current neighborhood supportive of your peace? If you are located in a city, are you finding ways to connect back to nature or your peace?

Harmony in the Workspace

If your work includes one physical workspace or office setting, take a moment to evaluate your workplace and ergonomics. Is the placement of your desk and height of your chair conducive to your working long hours? Working full-time indoors in a space without sunlight or fresh air may require the need to be intentional about breaks—preferably taken outside in nature with fresh air and sunshine.

Are you able to have access to healthy foods while you are working? Do you feel safe in both your neighborhood and your workplace? Do you allow *yourself* to take regular breaks and mentally withdraw your energy from your work?

Our relationships can reflect and align with the value we hold for ourselves. If we believe we are unworthy of boundaries, we will likely have no boundaries. If we don't prioritize ourselves, our work environments will reflect this back to us, which can be reflected in our salaries, relationships with our coworkers, or overloaded work responsibilities. We may find ourselves equating our self-value with our production levels or outputs. In place of feeling valuable within ourselves, we may run the risk of overreliance on the approval of others for our achievements. If any circumstances with coworkers leave you feeling that you are required to oversacrifice or overcompromise, are you willing to speak on it? Are you consistently taking on more weight in projects or responsibilities without tangible return? Do you believe it is inherently your responsibility to do so? There can be incremental burnout effects when we allow a routine of oversacrifice in the workplace.

Outro and Becoming Emboldened

Everybody, everybody wants to know
Where you going to
'Cause they wanna come
Or, so they think, until they find the cost of it
'Til they found out, found out what you lost for it
And I'll do it all again
'Cause I found love.
—Lauren Hill

When I first returned to Wilmington, I did something that I had been doing every visit since my dad passed away. I would go a little out of my way to drive down the street where his house had been. I would pause outside of the brick ivy-covered house that my grandparents built. One of the handful of memories I held was of being pulled in a red Radio Flyer wagon down this street by my dad. I used to love to go fast over the parts of the sidewalk fractured by the roots of magnolia trees. I remembered my younger self, weaving through the backyard, making calculated pitstops along the brick-laid path that my dad had laid. I would routinely stop at the overgrown honeysuckle bush and ascend up the hill to the fragrant banana shrub. I hold beautiful memories in my dad's yard with him, and looking back on these and other memories reminded me of the deep appreciation for nature that we both shared and our time spent there.

These gentle nudges to return to the house were like a north star, guiding me towards the part of myself in need of mending. I learned from this intentional heart-healing time that my happy memories had been suppressed at the cost of holding onto the painful parts. Through work and forgiveness, I found that the scales gradually came back into alignment, and that the positive memories carried their deserved weight, without being eclipsed. More than just thinking about these positive times, I let myself *feel* them again.

Before the wrapping up of this time, I had felt that routine pull to drive by and take in a glimpse of where his Volkswagen bug used to park and the diamond-paned windows, and then ride along—only to keep returning. Towards the end of my year in Wilmington, I stopped feeling the urgency of that pull. I do not feel that it is a coincidence that once I started tending to the needs of my inner child that the draw to return began to loosen. As I started showing up for myself, I stopped feeling a repeated pull to return—or to keep identifying with the pain. My story was being rewritten.

The Self-Love Journey (on Its Own)

In this process of our hearts being ideologically excavated, we are laying way for them to be built back up again and, this time, stronger than we recognize. Peeling back what lies within and loving these parts of ourselves can bring in genuine self-acceptance. A slow build of inner resilience is found, as we embrace these harder-to-face parts of ourselves and, we find, we can still survive. Self-acceptance is a powerful place to be.

When we are doing the work, each day brings an opportunity to move forward and continually evolve. A necessary self-love journey to pull us out of the trenches can eventually feel like a shallow pursuit if we are not sharing it with others. What begins as this internal and isolated track enables us to love others better and gratefully accept love. Also, it can hold the potential for us to align with our purpose and share this gift of self-acceptance with others.

Through performing the work to heal, we learn that self-love is a prerequisite and foundation for love. In healing, we have the opportunity to shed a chip, or boulder, that has invisibly rested rent-free on our shoulders and has tied us to past conditioning and limiting mind-sets. By knowing and honoring ourselves, we get the opportunity to exist from a more real and empowered place and find connection with a higher source.

Loving yourself enough has the power to get you on your purpose and prioritizing it. As you move forward from this place, you may gain grounding and strength from this renewed energy you give back to yourself. Through self-awareness and an awakened perspective, decisions aren't made from a place of casual default or unconscious decision-making.

In this fueling of intentional self-compassion, we continually acknowledge that our bodies, hearts, and minds are worth consistent investment. Through routine practice of investing in ourselves, we can build up greater self-empowerment. In the newfound place of living with greater authenticity and releasing self-abandonment, we show ourselves real love.

An awakening of who I had been in my relationships and who I was maturing into becoming temporarily left me feeling between two worlds. I could not fathom self-abandoning again. That cost had been too great. Also, I had become humbly aware of a divine guidance—guiding me, larger than me, and connected to me for which I am grateful. Whether intentionally or unconsciously, we are cocreating our course. Through conscious living and loving, we have this chance to cocreate, allowing ourselves to be guided from within. And no other relationship is worth more.

Tips Along Your Self-Love Journey

- Devote yourself daily to your practice of going within.
- Devote energy to your self-care.
- Be discerning with bringing your aspirations and insights to others.
- Don't waste your time and energy trying to convince someone of something.
- Do not entertain justification of behavior that hurts you.
- Try to release yourself from a timeline for your healing.
- Have compassion for yourself.

Old Story

- A belief that you are unworthy of love
- One where you are unloved
- One where you are a victim of how someone treated you and must remain stuck
- One where you need a person's validation of you
- One where joy cannot be found within you
- One where you keep yourself living small

New Story

- I am free to love and enjoy life.
- I am freeing myself from self-limiting beliefs.
- I am coming to accept abundant possibilities.
- I am free from fear.
- I am loved.
- I am living boldly and authentically.

Acknowledgments

I would like to thank my mom for continual writing check-ins and encouragement across decades. I thank my dad.

I love you both, deeply.

For the artistic and brave inspirations gained from their examples, thank you to Jessie Rehder, Marie Rehder Gerdes, and Katherine Rehder.

I am grateful for the lessons leading up to this point, and for the warriors working in the light who have encouraged my healing journey.

Endnotes

[1] W. E. Copeland, G. Keeler, A. Angold, and E. J. Costello. "Traumatic Events and Posttraumatic Stress in Childhood," *Archives of General Psychiatry* 64, no. 5 (2007): 577–584

[2] Bessel Van der Kolk, *The Body Keeps the Score* (New York: Penguin, 2014), 17.

[3] Bessel Van der Kolk, *The Body Keeps the Score* (New York: Penguin, 2014), 21.

[4] J. A. Astin, S. L. Shapiro, D. M. Eisenberg, and K. L. Forys. "Mind–Body Medicine: State of the Science, Implications for Practice," *Journal of American Board of Family Medicine* 16, no. 2 (2003): 131–147. And V. Brower, "Mind-Body Research Moves towards the Mainstream," *EMBO Reports* 7, no. 4 (2006): 358–361. doi:10.1038/sj.embor.7400671

[5] David Frawley, Dr. Subhash Ranade. *Ayurveda: Nature's Medicine* (Twin Lakes, WI: Lotus Press, 2001): 168

[6] Masuru Emoto. *The Hidden Messages of Water* (New York: Atria Press, 2005): xv.

[7] Masuru Emoto. *The Hidden Messages of Water* (New York: Atria Press, 2005): 77

[8] Masuru Emoto. *The Hidden Messages of Water* (New York: Atria Press, 2005): XX

[9] D. Church, et al., "Single-Session Reduction of the Intensity of Traumatic Memories in Abused Adolescents After EFT: A Randomized Controlled Pilot Study," *Traumatology* 18, no. 3 (2012): 73–79. And D. Feinstein and D. Church. "Modulating Gene Expression Through Psychotherapy: The Contribution of Noninvasive Somatic Interventions," *Review of General Psychology* 14, no. 4 (2010): 283–95.

[10] D. Feinstein. "Rapid Treatment of PTSD: Why Psychological Exposure with Acupoint Tapping May Be Effective," *Psychotherapy: Theory, Research, Practice, Training* 47, no. 3 (2010): 385–402. And D. Church, et al., "Psychological Trauma Symptom Improvement in Veterans Using EFT (Emotional Freedom Technique): A Randomized Controlled Trial," *Journal of Nervous and Mental Disease* 201 (2013): 153–160.

[11] L. Bernardi, P. Sleight, G. Bandinelli, S. Cencetti, et al. "Effect of Rosary Prayer and Yoga Mantras on Autonomic Cardiovascular Rhythms: Comparative Study," *BMJ* 323, no. 7327 (22–29 Dec 2001): 1446–1449.

[12] J. E. LeDoux. "Emotion Circuits in the Brain," *Annual Review of Neuroscience* 23 (2000): 155–184.

[13] Alberto A. Rasia-Filho, Renata Gomes Londero, Matilde Achaval. *Journal of Psychiatry & Neuroscience* (2000).

[14] Tang et. al. "Short-Term Meditation Training Improves Attention and Self-Regulation," *Proc Nat'l Acad Sci USA* (2007). doi: 10.1073/pnas.0707678104

[15] K. W. Brown, R. M. Ryan, and J. D. Creswell. "Mindfulness: Theoretical Foundations and Evidence for Its Salutary Effects," *Psychological Inquiry* 18, no. 4 (2007): 211–237. doi: 10.1080/10478400701598298

[16] J. Greeson, and J. Brantley. "Mindfulness and Anxiety Disorders: Developing a Wise Relationship with the Inner Experience of Fear," *Clinical Handbook of Mindfulness* (New York, NY: Springer Science, 2009): 171–188).

[17] R. J. Davidson, J. Kabat-Zinn, J. Schumacher, M. Rosenkranz, D. Muller, S. F. Santorelli, and J. F. Sheridan. "Alterations in Brain and Immune Function Produced by Mindfulness Meditation," *Psychosomatic Medicine* 65, no. 4 (2003): 564–570.

[18] D. S. Ludwig, and J. Kabat-Zinn. "Mindfulness in Medicine," *The Journal of the American Medical Association* 300, no. 11(2008): 1350–1352.

[19] K. W. Brown, R. M. Ryan, and J. D. Creswell. "The Effects of Mindfulness-Based Stress Reduction on Sleep Disturbance: A Systematic Review," *Journal of Science and Healing* 3, no. 6(2007): 585–591.

[20] Amy Weintraub. *Yoga Skills for Therapists* (New York W. W. Norton and Company, 2012): 162.

[21] C. Streeter, et al. "Yoga Asana Sessions Increase Brain GABA Levels: A Pilot Study," *The Journal of Alternative and Complementary Medicine* 13, no. 4 (2007): 419–426

[22] P. Tekur, R. Nagarathna, S. Chametcha, A. Hankey, H. R. Nagendra. "A Comprehensive Yoga Programs Improves Pain, Anxiety and Depression in Chronic Low Back Pain Patients More Than Exercise: An RCT," *Complementary Therapies in Medicine* 20, no. 3 (2012):107–118.

[23] S. G. Hofmann, A. T. Sawyer, A. A. Witt, and D. Oh. "The Effect of Mindfulness-Based Therapy on Anxiety and Depression: A Meta-Analytic Review," *Journal of Consulting and Clinical Psychology* 78, no. 2 (2010):169–183

[24] L. Bernardi, P. Sleight, G. Bandinelli, S. Cencetti, et al. "Effect of Rosary Prayer and Yoga Mantras on Autonomic Cardiovascular

Rhythms: Comparative Study," *BMJ* 323, no. 7327 (22–29 Dec 2001): 1446–1449. https://www.ncbi.nlm.nih.gov/pubmed/11751348

[25] Amy Weintraub. *Yoga Skills for Therapists* (New York W. W. Norton and Company, 2012): 100

[26] V. Arvind, L. Cano, and A. Kavya. Effect of alkaline diet and pH on chronic pain. Poster presentation at PAINWeek, September 6, 2013, Las Vegas, NV. Poster 3745.

[27] J. Vormann, M. Worlitschek., T. Goedecke., and B. Silver B. "Supplementation with Alkaline Minerals Reduces Symptoms in Patients with Chronic Lower Back Pain," *J Trace Elem Med Biol* 15, no. 2–3 (2001):179–183.

About the Author

Catherine Gerdes is a Certified Integrative Health Coach trained at Duke Integrative Medicine and trained in Ayurvedic Health Coaching. She is the founder of the Wellthy Coach and coaches clients along their wellness journeys towards transforming their mindset, achieving their wellness goals and healing through mindfulness practices. Catherine is also a Registered Yoga Teacher who happily finds her recharge at the beach. She gives gratitude to Spirit for all things.

NOTES

NOTES

NOTES

NOTES

NOTES

NOTES

Lightning Source UK Ltd.
Milton Keynes UK
UKHW012024131120
373373UK00010B/776/J